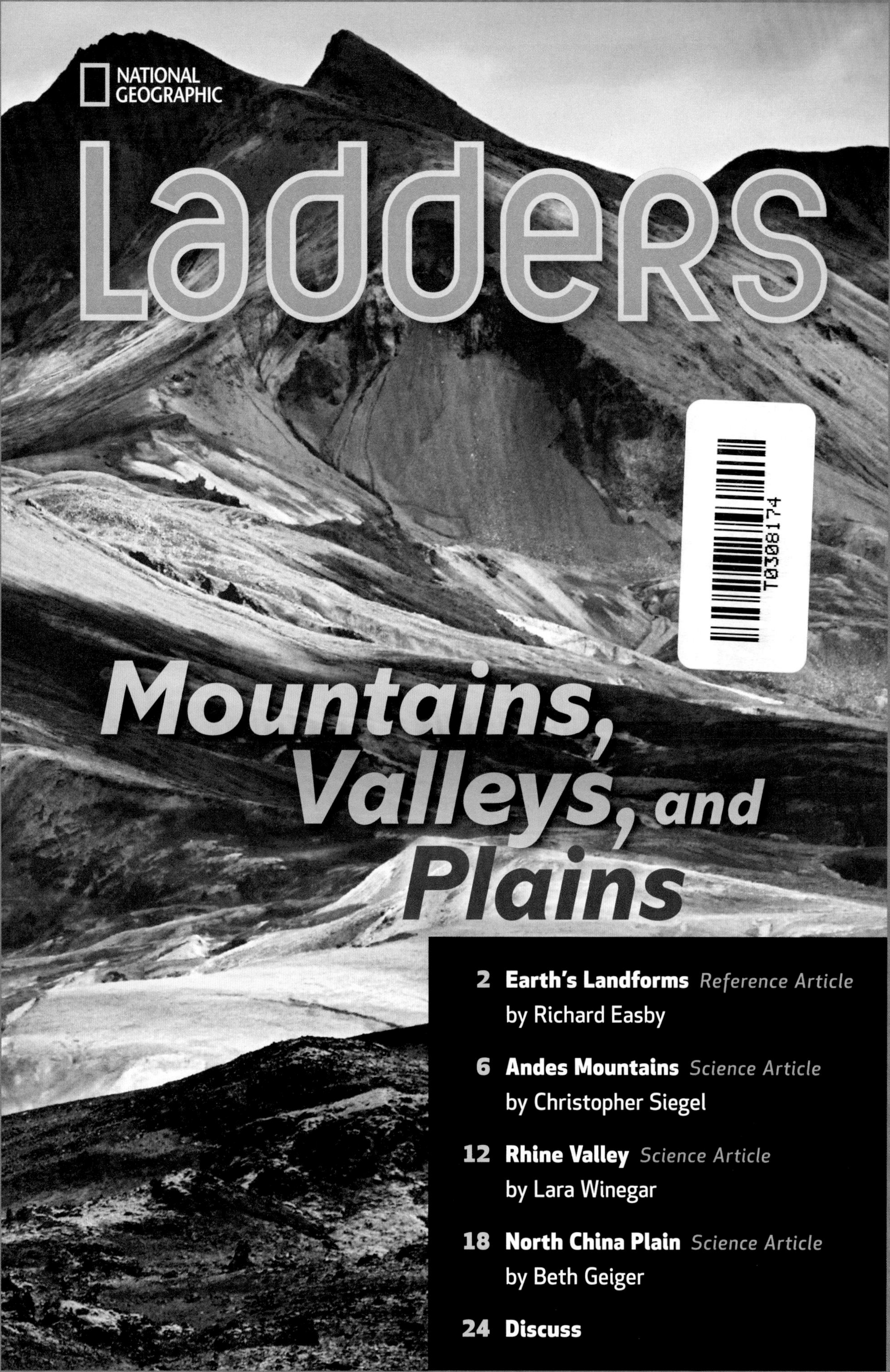

NATIONAL GEOGRAPHIC

Ladders

Mountains, Valleys, and Plains

GENRE Reference Article

Read to find out about Earth's landforms.

EARTH LAND

by Richard Easby

Imagine you are in an airplane flying high above Earth. Looking down, you see the amazing features of our planet. In some places, high **mountains** reach for the sky. Their snow-covered peaks look like ice cream cones. They can be cold, windswept places where few plants and animals survive. In other areas deep, wide **valleys** snake their way across the land. Many valleys have rivers running along the bottom. Farther on, you see flat **plains** stretching to the horizon. Some are sandy deserts. Others look like seas of grass. It's time to put your feet back on the ground and get to know some of Earth's wonderful **landforms.**

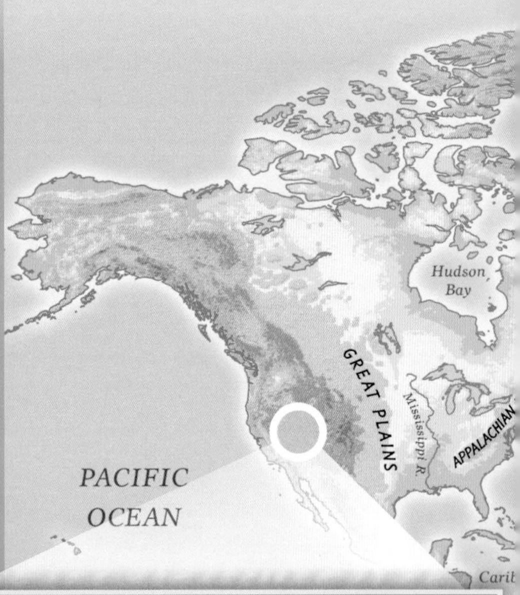

Rocky Mountains

A mountain is a very high place with steep sides.

The Rocky Mountains stretch between the United States and Canada. Some of its peaks are over 4,267 meters (14,000 feet) high.

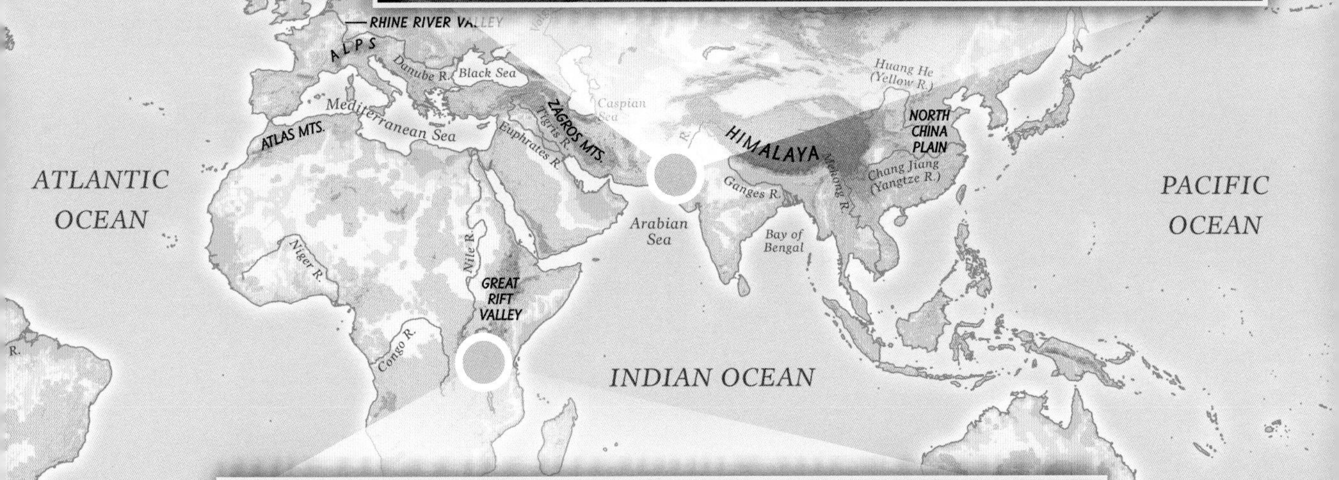

Indus Valley

A valley is a low land bordered by higher land.

The Indus Valley is in Asia. The valley was shaped by the Indus River. It stretches nearly 3,000 kilometers (1,864 miles), across the countries of India and Pakistan, to the Arabian Sea. The valley is the site of some of Earth's earliest civilizations.

Serengeti Plain

A plain is a large, flat area of land.

The Serengeti Plain stretches across the countries of Kenya and Tanzania in Africa. It is a large, flat grassland. Herds of zebras, elephants, lions, and other wildlife live on the plain.

Prepare yourself! You are about to embark on an exploration of three of the most intriguing destinations on the planet. We'll begin by visiting the Andes Mountains, South America's longest mountain range. Next we'll travel to the Rhine River Valley, one of Europe's largest valleys and a center of transportation, farming, and industry. Finally, we'll visit Asia's North China Plain, one of the most populated places on Earth. You'll discover how these landforms were shaped by nature. You'll also learn what it's like to live in each of these unique places.

North China Plain

Andes Mountains

The Andes are high, rugged mountains. The peaks are often sharp and jagged. The Andes stretch from Venezuela in the north to Argentina in the south. Nestled within the mountains are remains of ancient civilizations, including the Inca.

Rhine Valley

The flowing waters of the Rhine River formed the Rhine Valley. The river begins as a fast moving mountain stream in Switzerland. It travels through Germany, France, and the Netherlands forming, a wide valley containing rich farmland.

North China Plain

The North China Plain is a vast, flat area. The plain consists of deep layers of sediments deposited by rivers such as the Huang He. Much of the plain is used for farmland, but the modern city of Beijing is located on its northern edge.

Check In Compare and contrast mountains, valleys, and plains.

GENRE Science Article

Read to find out about the Andes Mountains.

ANDES MOUNTAINS

by Christopher Siegel

HOLA Y BIENVENIDOS A LA CORDILLERA DE LOS ANDES!

Hello and welcome to the Andes Mountains!

Look around you, but don't make yourself dizzy by the height! You are on top of some of the world's tallest **mountains**—the Andes Mountains. Some of the towering summits soar to 6,100 meters (20,000 feet) above sea level.

Not only are the Andes some of the tallest mountains in the world, they make up one of the longest groups of mountains. The Andes extend for about 7,000 kilometers (4,350 miles) over much of the continent of South America.

Look closely at the mountain peaks. You will notice that the rock is rough and jagged. Some mountains have pointed tops and sharp ridges that connect the peaks. Ice created many of these rocky formations in a process called **weathering.** Water freezes in cracks in rock. As the water turns to ice, it expands. This causes the rock to split apart. The result is the beautiful rocky mountain peaks that surround you.

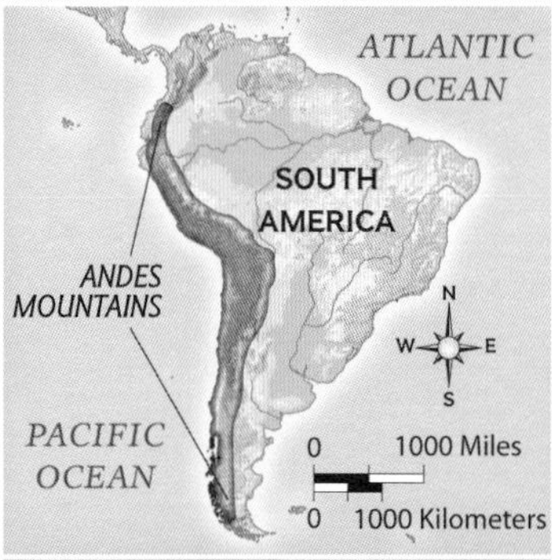

The Andes are located in South America.

Water seeps into the cracks of rocks. When the water freezes, it expands. This causes the rock to break apart.

LIVING IN THE MOUNTAINS

CLIMATE

High in the Andes, the air is often cold and dry. The highest peaks have snow year round. The weather doesn't change much from season to season.

TRANSPORTATION

Mountains naturally have steep slopes and the rock is constantly breaking apart and wearing away. The loose rock can create dangerous landslides in the mountains.

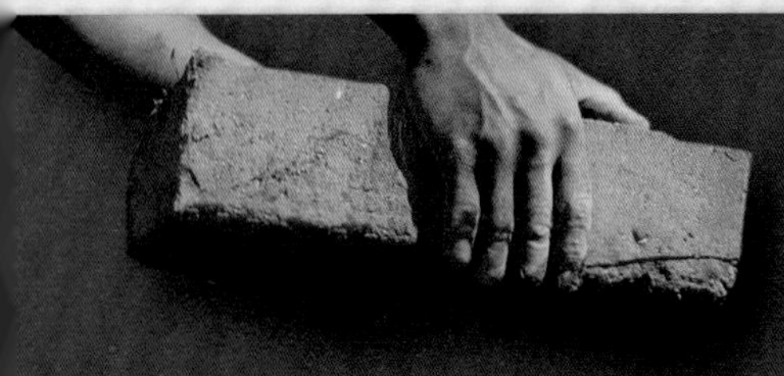

WHERE PEOPLE LIVE

The Andes Mountains are rocky with very thin soil. Although grasses and some crops can grow in this environment, the thin soil and cold climate make it hard for trees to grow.

People living high in the mountains need warm clothes almost year round. Most traditional clothes are made from alpaca fiber.

Moving about on the mountains isn't always easy. Motor vehicles can have a hard time on the steep slopes. Driving can be dangerous! Many people get around on foot or use pack animals to carry their goods and supplies.

People living high in the Andes build their homes and other buildings using the **natural resources** around them. Most buildings are constructed using stone and clay soil. The clay is used to make adobe bricks.

ALPACAS

Since ancient times, the Andes have been the home to a herd animal called an alpaca. Alpaca fleece, the animals' soft outer coat, was prized by the ancient Incan civilization. It was called the "fiber of the gods." Looking out in the mountainous Andes landscape, today, you will still see herds of alpacas. Like the ancient Inca, people use the fleece to make hats, ponchos, blankets, and other woven items.

1. HERDING Alpacas are herd animals and generally like to stay together. Herds are watched over by their owners, much in the same way a shepherd watches over sheep.

2. SHEARING Alpacas are sheared at least once a year. The fleece is removed from the animal and it eventually grows back. It's much like a haircut.

3. DYEING Alpaca fleece can be dyed into a rainbow of colors. Many dyes are made from plants that grow in the Andes.

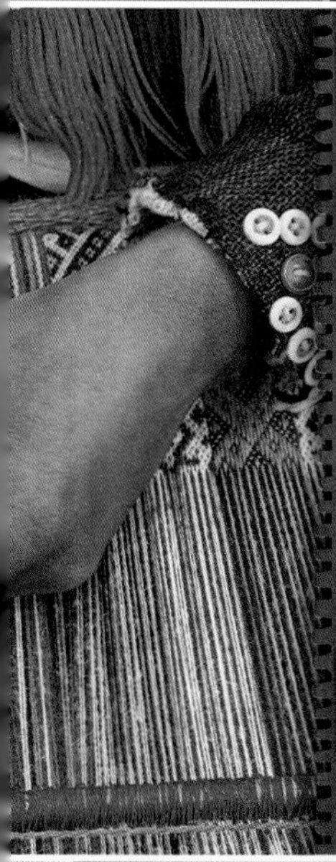

4. KNITTING AND WEAVING Alpaca fiber is spun together into threads of yarn. The yarn is then knitted or woven into cloth and other fabrics. Many colorful items are made from the yarn.

5. AT THE MARKET Markets and local shops throughout the Andes sell items made of alpaca fiber. The woven clothes are popular with local people and with tourists visiting the region.

Check In How are the Andes different from where you live?

GENRE Science Article

Read to find out about the Rhine Valley.

Rhine Valley

by Lara Winegar

Hallo und Willkommen zum Rhein-Tal!

Hello and welcome to the Rhine Valley!

Looking down into the **valley** you can see that this is one beautiful place. It is an area dotted with ancient castles, modern cities, small villages, and rich farmland. The Rhine Valley is one of Europe's most famous and most visited areas.

The valley was formed by the Rhine River, which flows roughly north for about 1,300 kilometers (800 miles). The river starts in Switzerland as a small mountain stream. As the river reaches flatter ground, it broadens and the water slows down. Over time, the moving water eroded the land and formed a wide valley. **Erosion** is the picking up and moving of rocks and soil to a new place.

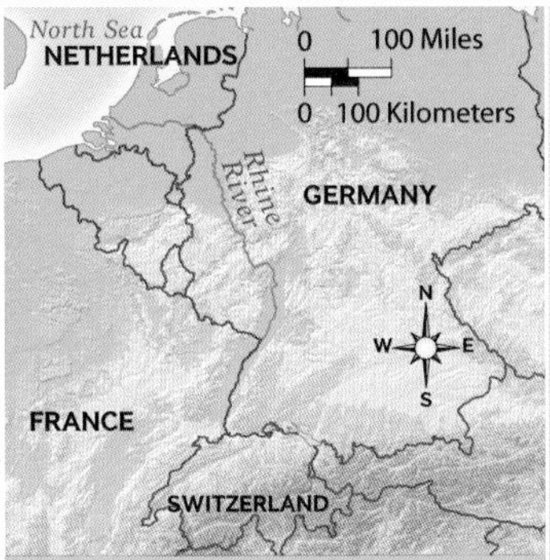

The Rhine Valley follows the Rhine River, which flows through much of Europe.

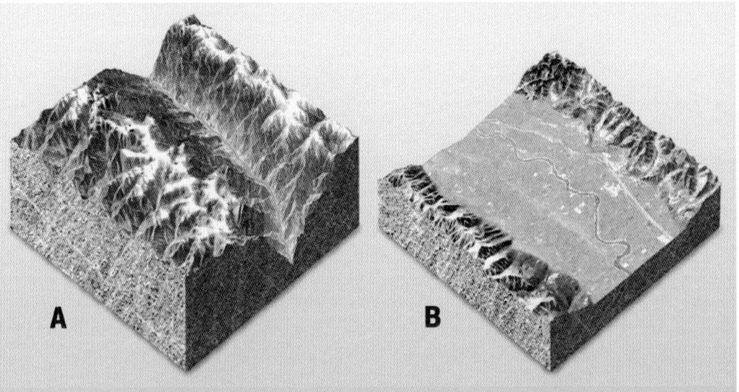

Over time, the rushing waters of the Rhine River formed the Rhine Valley. The valley starts out narrow and steep (A). It becomes broad as the river crosses flatter land (B).

Living in the Valley

Climate

The landscape of the Rhine Valley changes with the seasons. Most of the valley experiences warm, humid summers; cool, dry autumns; cold winters; and warm, wet springs.

Transportation

The Rhine River has been a major transportation route since the valley was first settled. The river links southern and northern Europe. Boats carry goods and materials to cities and towns along the river.

Where People Live

The water of the Rhine River is one of the region's most important **natural resources.** People living in the valley rely on water from the river to use in their homes, on their farms, and for making products. People originally settled along the river for its reliable supply of water.

Snow in the Rhine Valley and the surrounding **mountains** is common throughout the winter season. The snow makes winter sports, such as skiing, possible. Children enjoy playing in the snow, too!

The flat valley floor provides an ideal surface for transportation routes. Roads connect the many settlements in the Rhine Valley. High speed trains carry passengers and goods from one place to another.

Centuries ago, castles were built along the Rhine River to protect the surrounding land and for easy access to water. As more people began to live in the region, villages and eventually towns and cities developed.

Flowers

The Rhine Valley is just right for growing flowers. Water from the river irrigates the land and the region's soil is rich and fertile. When in bloom, rows of flowers, including the Netherland's famous tulips, make a patchwork of brightly colored fields.

1. PLANTING Tulip bulbs are best planted in the fall before the ground is frozen. The plants begin to grow underground and eventually push to the surface in spring.

2. GROWING Flowers, including tulips, are grown in vast fields. The flowers need a lot of water as they grow. Machines are used to spray water and fertilizer onto the plants. The flowers are harvested just before they bloom.

3. HARVESTING Flowers are harvested and sent to market very quickly. The cut flowers need to be kept in water and in a cool place to keep them from wilting and drying out.

4. SELLING Cut flowers from the Rhine Valley, especially from the Netherlands, are sold in local markets, and they are also sent overseas. The flowers you buy in your local market may have been grown in the Rhine Valley.

Check In How is the Rhine Valley different from where you live?

GENRE Science Article

Read to find out about the North China Plain.

North China Plain

by Beth Geiger

欢迎华北平原

Welcome to the North China Plain!

Look around. You can see far into the distance. There are no towering **mountains** or other landforms to spoil the view of the **plain.** But don't let your eyes deceive you! The North China Plain is not all the same. Some areas include large cities with tall skyscrapers. Other areas are dry, rocky deserts, and still, other areas of the plain are farmlands.

What on Earth could make such a vast, flat **landform**? The answer is tiny particles of Earth materials called silt.

Over millions of years the surrounding rocky highlands were **weathered** or broken down into smaller and smaller pieces until they became silt. The silt **eroded** and was carried from the highlands by rivers and streams, including the Huang He. When the rivers flooded, they deposited, or dropped, the silt on the surrounding land.

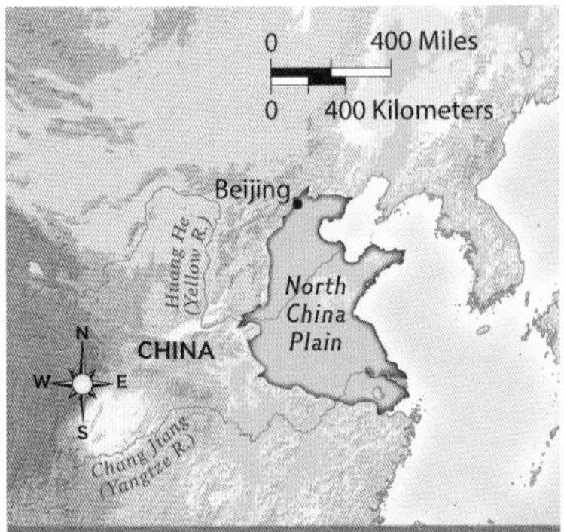

The North China Plain is a large flat area in China.

The North China Plain was formed over a long period of time. Rivers deposited layers of silt on Earth's surface like a blanket spread out over the land.

Living on the Plain

CLIMATE

Climate in the North China Plain region varies. Some parts are arid, or dry, with little rainfall. Other parts of the North China Plain experience massive flooding almost every year.

TRANSPORTATION

The North China Plain is a vast expanse of land. It makes up a large portion of the country of China. Given the area's vast expanse, people use different forms of transportation.

WHERE PEOPLE LIVE

A large part of the world's population lives on or near the North China Plain. The places where people live are very different. Some live in rural villages.

Floods can be dangerous to people, so dams have been built along the Huang He. Dams control the flow of water, but they also block the silt carried by the river. This results in less silt being deposited on the plain.

People living a long way from major cities often rely on traditional forms of transport such as bicycles, horses, or even camels. Modern high-speed trains and paved roads for automobiles connect towns and cities.

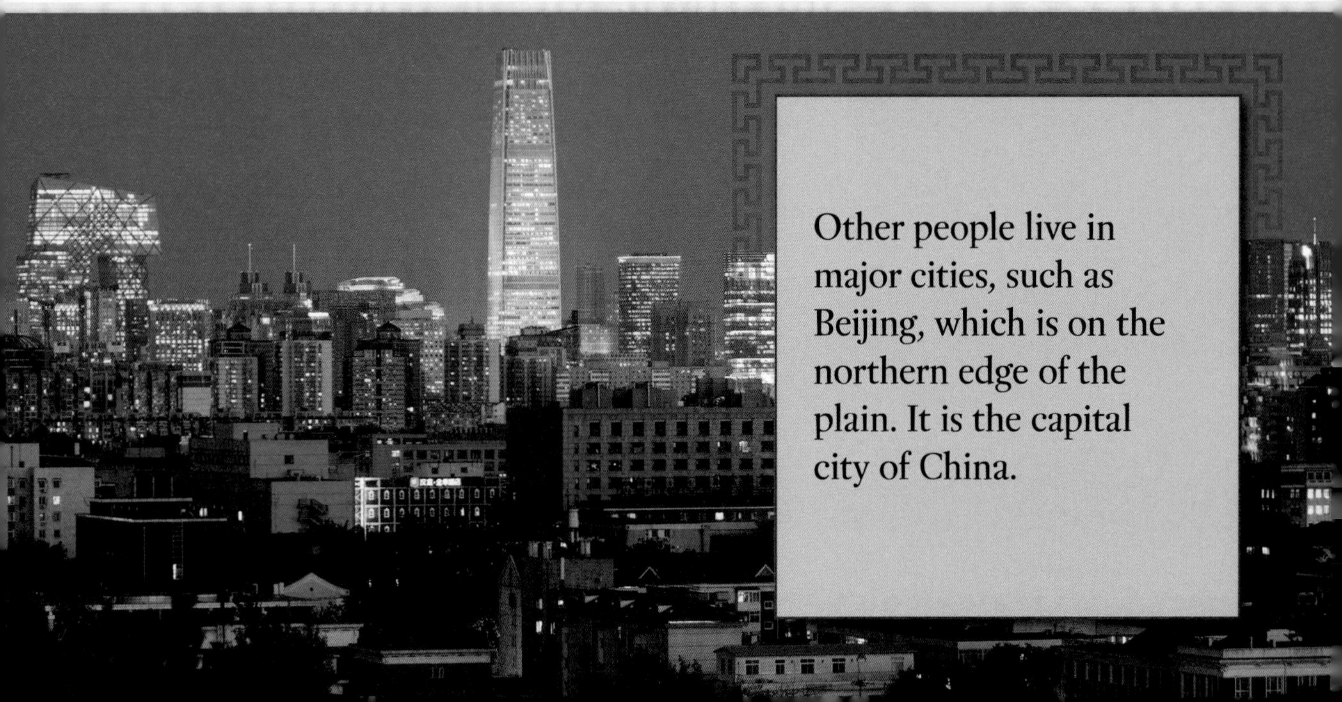

Other people live in major cities, such as Beijing, which is on the northern edge of the plain. It is the capital city of China.

Cotton

The silt left behind by flooding has created a fertile, or rich, soil for crops. Many food crops are grown on the North China Plain such as wheat, millet, and corn. Another important crop is cotton. Cotton is used to make clothes and other goods. China is one of the world's leading producers of cotton.

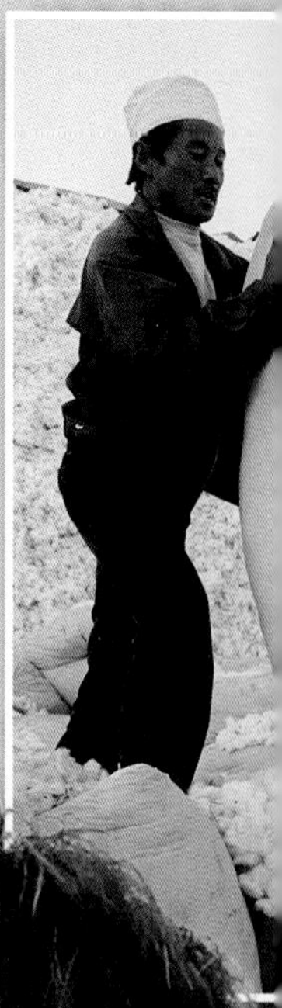

1. PLANTING Cotton seeds are planted in rows. The plants grow into pyramid- or cone-shaped plants about 1–2 meters (3–6 feet) tall. The plants need plenty of water and sunlight to grow and produce cotton. It takes a cotton plant about 200 days from planting until the cotton is ready for harvesting.

2. HARVESTING The cotton is ready to be harvested when it looks like small white clouds. After the cotton is picked, it is bundled into bales. Truckloads of cotton bales are then transported to factories for processing.

3. PROCESSING Processing the cotton takes many steps. After being cleaned, the cotton fibers are spun into cotton yarn. This looks like ropes of cotton fiber. Eventually the cotton is spun into thread.

4. PRODUCING GOODS Cotton is used to make many different goods, including clothes, such as jeans. Most goods have a tag attached. The tag states what the item was made from and where. Many goods are made of cotton from the North China Plain.

Check In How is the North China Plain different from where you live?

Discuss

1. Compare the three landforms discussed in this book. How are mountains, valleys, and plains different from each other? How are they similar?

2. What are the different natural resources you read about in this book? Describe how these resources are used.

3. What place described in this book would you most like to visit? Why?

4. What do you still wonder about these places? Where could you go to find more information?